# Moments of Refreshing
## Bruce T. Howard, Jr.

Published in the United States by Bruce T. Howard Ministries LLC

Paperback ISBN: 979-8-218-87812-2

eBook ISBN: 979-8-218-87811-5

LCCN: 2025926600

Credits:
Cover Photographer: Riddell T. Gardner, Sr.
Creative Designer: DeSean M. Wright
Proofreader: Marquita ShaNa Blair
Editorial and Production Manager: Angelo K. Walker

The Cataloging-in-Publication Data is on file with the Library of Congress.

This book is available at special quantity discounts when purchased in bulk by corporations, organizations, and special-interest groups. For more information or permissions, contact: brucethoward.com

This devotional is lovingly dedicated to those whose lives have shaped, inspired, and strengthened me along this journey of faith.

**To my maternal grandparents, Pastor Willie O. and Mrs. Eva Little**—my childhood pastors and spiritual foundation. Your love, prayers, and faithful example continue to guide me, and your support towards my mother helped shape us with wisdom, discipline, and grace.

To my **biological father, Mr. Bruce T. Howard Sr.**, who transitioned from this life on *January 5, 2024.* Though you are no longer here in the physical, your presence, legacy, and love remain alive in my heart.

To my mother, **Mrs. Evenda Stephens,** and my **dad, Reverend Izell Stephens,** thank you for your unwavering love, guidance, and faith. You have been my earthly examples of strength, perseverance, and godly love.

To my **sister, Elysea Stuckey, brother-in-law, Dr. Jaroy Stuckey**, and my precious **nephew and niece, AJ and Eva Stuckey**, whose lives were tragically taken far too soon. Your memory lives on, and your love continues to refresh my spirit daily. You are forever missed and eternally cherished.

To my **beautiful wife, Mrs. Gabrielle Howard**, my greatest supporter and partner in purpose—thank you for believing in this vision and in me. And to our precious **daughter, Adalynn Grace Howard**, and our loving doggy daughter, **Bella**, you both bring joy, laughter, and balance to my life each day.

## Preface

The vision for *Moments of Refreshing* was birthed in the year 2020—a time when the world was gripped by uncertainty, fear, and isolation. During the global pandemic, God placed it on my heart to create a space where people could gather for spiritual renewal and hope. Out of that divine prompting, a weekly prayer call known as **"The Refreshing"** was born. Every Wednesday morning at 7 AM, believers from various places would connect to pray, reflect, and be strengthened by the Word of God. Those sacred moments became wells of living water in a dry and weary season.

From those early mornings of prayer and connection, the Lord impressed upon me the importance of continuing this assignment beyond the call. Thus, *Moments of Refreshing* was created—a daily devotional designed to refresh both your **mind and spirit.** Each devotion is written to offer encouragement, insight, and inspiration for your journey.

In addition to reading, you will find reflective questions after each devotion. These are intentional moments for you to pause, ponder, and personally apply what you've read. It's in these quiet reflections that transformation takes root and true refreshing occurs.

My prayer is that as you journey through these pages, you will experience renewal in every area of your life. May each devotion draw you closer to God, rekindle your faith, and remind you that even in life's driest seasons—God always provides **moments of refreshing.**

**— Bruce T. Howard, Jr.**
*Author & Servant of The Refreshing*

# CONTENTS

# Day 1: The Lord Is With You

Scripture: "The Lord is my shepherd; I shall not want." (Psalm 23:1 KJV)

**Devotional Message:**

In a world full of change, it's a profound comfort to know that God remains the same. People and circumstances may shift, but His faithfulness, presence, and power never waver. Today's scripture, Psalm 23:1, offers a powerful reminder: "The Lord is my shepherd; I shall not want."

To say, "The Lord is my shepherd," is to declare that God is your protector, your guide, and your provider. He hasn't forgotten you. He knows exactly where you are and what you are facing. He is not a distant figure but is intimately close. He sees your heart, hears every prayer, and understands every need. When your strength feels low and the days feel long, remember this truth: because He is your Shepherd, you have everything you need.

Let this be your anchor today. The Lord is...

- My Shepherd: He watches over you and never leaves your side.

- My Provider: He meets every need, even the ones you haven't spoken aloud

- My Peace: In moments of quiet and chaos, He offers rest for your soul

- My Comfort: In loneliness or pain, He walks beside you.

You are not forgotten. You are not alone. You are deeply loved by the Shepherd of your soul.

**Reflection Questions:**

- **Understanding the Shepherd:**
    - What does it mean to you that God is your "shepherd"? How does this image bring you comfort or peace?
    - Think about a time when you felt like you "shall not want" because of God's provision. What was that experience like?
- **Personal Reflection:**
    - In what specific area of your life do you need to be reminded that God is your shepherd and provider?
    - How can you intentionally rest in His presence today, trusting that He is your peace and comfort?

**Devotional Prayer:**

Heavenly Father, thank You for being my Shepherd. Thank You for Your unwavering presence and for always being everything I need. Today, I ask that You remind me that You are near. Help me to trust in Your guidance and find rest in Your peace. In Jesus' name, Amen.

**Notes:**

_____

_____

_____

# Day 2: I Am Pregnant With Purpose

Scripture: "Now to Him who is able to do immeasurably more than all we ask or imagine, according to His power that is at work within us, to Him be glory in the church and in Christ Jesus throughout all generations, forever and ever! Amen." (Ephesians 3:20-21 NIV)

**Devotional Message:**

You are not ordinary; you are carrying something extraordinary! God has planted a divine purpose within you, powered by His greatness. Every insecurity, obstacle, and doubt that tries to arise is no match for the power of God working inside you. Like a mother carrying a child, this purpose must be nurtured and protected.

It may not always be visible, and at times you may doubt its presence, especially when faced with life's challenges. However, understand that your purpose is far beyond what you can conceive or even imagine God himself has equipped you with His limitless power to overcome every insecurity and obstacle. Knowing this, you can walk boldly with confidence and authority.

Every step you take is a declaration of His glory. Your journey is unique and significant. You are not here by accident but by divine design. Whether in moments of triumph or trials, know that each instant is shaping you to fulfill your heavenly calling. You are pregnant with God's purpose, and your life is a reflection of His power and promise.

*Make These Daily Declarations:*

- I am confident in Christ's power within me.
- I know who I am and the greatness I carry.
- I defeat insecurity and every obstacle by acknowledging God's greatness in me.
- I walk boldly with divine authority and purpose.
- I am a living reflection of God's power and promise!

**Reflection Questions:**

- **Understanding Purpose:**
    - What does it mean to be "pregnant with purpose" in the context of this devotional?
    - How does recognizing God's power within you change your perspective on your purpose?

- **Personal Reflection:**
    - Can you identify a moment in your life where you felt particularly aware of a purpose that God has placed within you? Write about this experience.
    - What obstacles or insecurities have you faced that might have hindered your journey towards this purpose? How have you or how can you overcome them?

**Devotional Prayer:**

Father, I am humbled and grateful for the extraordinary purpose You have planted within me, powered by Your immeasurable greatness. As I face life's insecurities and obstacles, remind me that nothing can stand against Your mighty power at work in me. Empower me to walk with boldness, confidence, and divine authority, knowing that I am pregnant with purpose and reflecting Your glory with every step I take. Let my life be a true testament to Your promises and a beacon of hope to the world. In Jesus' name, Amen.

**Notes:**

_____

_____

_____

# Day 3: Leveling Up to Rule and Reign

Scripture: "Therefore, since we are surrounded by such a great cloud of witnesses, let us throw off everything that hinders and the sin that so easily entangles. And let us run with perseverance the race marked out for us." (Hebrews 12:1 NIV)

**Devotional Message:**

God is extending a divine invitation to "level up" in our spiritual walk. This isn't just about growing older; it's about maturing in our faith through obedience, trust, and action. God has called us to rise as believers and take hold of the authority and purpose He has already given us.

God has a specific assignment for you: *to spread the life-changing message of Jesus Christ.* The question is whether you will step into that calling. To rule and reign, you must let go of what's holding you back. What is weighing you down? It could be sin, fear, unhealthy relationships, or doubt. Letting go requires intentionality and courage, but it is the only way to move forward and embrace the spiritual growth God desires for you. Leveling up means taking your faith to a new height. This involves:

- Rising in prayer: Deepen your relationship with God by prioritizing time in His presence.
- Walking in boldness: Don't shy away from opportunities to share the Gospel or live out your faith.
- Embracing responsibility: Accept the assignment God has given you with a heart of gratitude and determination.

God is calling you to live above mediocrity and take your rightful place as His ambassador. You were made to rule and reign. Not as a dictator, but as a humble servant of Christ, leading others to Him. Don't wait until tomorrow to fulfill your purpose. Begin now. Every day is a gift, and every opportunity is a chance to make an eternal impact.

**Reflection Questions:**

- **Personal Inventory:**

  - Hebrews 12:1 talks about "throwing off everything that hinders." What is one specific weight or sin you need to let go of to level up spiritually?
  - How does the idea of being "destined for greatness" and having a personal assignment from God impact your perspective on your daily life?

- **Action and Application:**

  - In which of the three areas: prayer, boldness, or responsibility, do you feel God is calling you to take a "level up" step before the year ends?
  - What is one bold step you can take this week to begin fulfilling your God-given assignment?

**Devotional Prayer:**

Heavenly Father, thank You for calling us to rule and reign as Your children. Help us to remember You in all we do and to rise to the occasion as believers. Give us the strength to let go of anything hindering our growth and the boldness to walk in the greatness You've destined for us. As we close out this year, may we step into the new year ready to fulfill our assignment and glorify You in everything. In Jesus' name, Amen.

**Notes:**

_____

_____

_____

# Day 4: Are You Ready?

Scripture: "But of that day and hour knoweth no man, no, not the angels of heaven, but my Father only." (Matthew 24:36 KJV)

**Devotional Message:**

"Are you ready?" This isn't just a simple question; it's a wake-up call for every believer. Jesus made it clear in Matthew 24:36 that no one, not even the angels or the Son, knows the day or hour of His return, but only the Father. This means every day we live is a precious opportunity to prepare for eternity.

This life is not the final destination. It's the dressing room before the main event, the rehearsal before the performance, the preparation before the promise. With that in mind, have you truly prepared for His return?

In a world filled with distractions, busy schedules and endless responsibilities, we must not lose sight of our most important priority: living in readiness for Christ's return. This means:

- Be fervent in prayer: Prayer is not optional; it is the lifeline that connects you to God.
- Stay in intercession: Stand in the gap for others. Seek His face for your family, your community, and even your enemies.
- Check your priorities: Are your priorities in divine order? Is your heart aligned with His will?
- Live holy: Strive not for perfection but for a pure heart and consistent obedience and repentance.
- Treat people right: Your love walk matters. Jesus said the world would know we are His disciples by our love for one another.

Every word you speak, every action you take, and every choice you make is part of your preparation. It is your call to stay ready. The trumpet could sound at any moment. Are you watching? Are you praying? Are you living as if today might be your last?

**Reflection Questions:**

- **Are You Prepared?**

  - If Christ were to return today, what would He find you doing?
  - How would you describe your current state of readiness for His return? What is one area you feel you need to improve?

- **Your Priorities:**

  - What are some of the biggest distractions that keep you from living with eternity in mind?
  - How can you realign your daily priorities to better reflect a life of readiness for Christ?

**Devotional Prayer:**

Lord, help me to live each day with eternity in mind. Stir up a fervent spirit within me to pray, to intercede and to walk in holiness. Teach me to treat others with love, grace, and compassion. Let nothing in this world distract me from preparing for Your return. In Jesus' name, Amen.

**Notes:**

_____

_____

_____

# Day 5: The Reward of Risk

Scripture: "Come,' he said. Then Peter got down out
of the boat, walked on the water and came toward Jesus."
(Matthew 14:29 NIV)

**Devotional Message:**

Peter's decision to step out of the boat was a significant risk,
but it was a risk rooted in faith. He could have stayed in the
perceived safety of the boat with the other disciples. He
stepped out in faith, answering the call of Jesus instead. In
that moment of obedience, he experienced something
miraculous; he walked on water!

This powerful story teaches us that faith often requires us to
take risks. Whether it's stepping into a new opportunity,
pursuing a God-given dream, or simply trusting Him in
uncertain times, risks are often the doorway to extraordinary
rewards. You may feel a pull toward a new direction, but fear,
doubt, or the comfort of your current situation may try to
hold you back. Remember, when a risk is motivated by faith
and obedience to God, the reward on the other side is far
greater than the comfort you leave behind.

Keep pushing forward. Step out in faith, and trust that God is
waiting for you on the other side of your obedience. The risk
is worth the reward!

**Reflection Questions:**

- **Taking a Risk:**

    - The boat represented Peter's safety and comfort. What "boat" might you be holding onto that God is calling you to step out of?
    - What is one specific risk you feel God is asking you to take in your life right now?

- **Trust and Obedience:**

    - In what area of your life do you need to place more trust in Jesus, even if it feels uncertain or scary?
    - How does the knowledge that God is waiting for you on the "other side of your obedience" change your perspective on taking a risk?

**Devotional Prayer:**

Heavenly Father, thank You for the example of Peter, who took a risk and trusted in Your call. Give me the courage to step out of my own "boat" of comfort and fear. Strengthen my faith to trust You in uncertain times and to pursue the dreams and opportunities You have placed in my heart. I know that the reward of my obedience is far greater than any risk I might take. In Jesus' name, Amen.

**Notes:**

_____

_____

_____

# Day 6: Faith In Muddy Water

Scripture: "For we walk by faith, not by sight." (2 Corinthians 5:7 KJV)

**Devotional Message:**

It's easy to have faith when the water is clear, when we can see the bottom, when the path ahead is well-lit, and when every step is on solid ground. In these moments of clarity and certainty, confidence comes naturally. But the true test of our faith isn't found in the calm and the clarity; it's found in the mud.

What do you do when life gets murky? When a diagnosis comes back uncertain, when a job falls through, when trusted relationships crumble, or when your vision is clouded and your steps are unsure? Can you still believe when you can't see? Can you still stand when the ground is soft beneath your feet? Can you still have faith in muddy water?

In the mud, everything slows down. It's difficult to move and it's easy to get stuck. But the mud is also where God often does some of His greatest work. Just like a seed that grows underground: covered in dirt, in darkness, and surrounded by pressure, just know something is becoming in the mess! Your faith is becoming. Your endurance is becoming. Your testimony is being formed in the very place that feels messy and unclear.

Jesus never promised that every step would be easy but He did promise to be with us. And if He's with you in the mud, you're not just surviving; you're becoming. You are developing a faith that isn't based on what you can see, but on Who you trust.

**Reflection Questions:**

- **Navigating the Mud:**

    - What area of your life feels "muddy" or unclear right now?
    - How has God shown Himself faithful to you during unclear seasons in the past? What did you learn about Him and yourself?

- **Trust and Becoming:**

    - How does the idea that God is developing something in you "in the mud" change your perspective on your current struggles?
    - What is one practical step you can take today to choose faith over-sight in your current situation?

**Devotional Prayer:**

Lord, sometimes the water is muddy and I don't know which way to go. But today, I choose to trust You even when I can't see. Strengthen my faith in the muddy moments. Help me to remember that even in the mess, You are making something beautiful. I am convinced that right here, in the thick of it all, I am becoming exactly who You called me to be. In Jesus' name, Amen.

**Notes:**

_____

_____

_____

# Day 7: It Is What It Is, but It's Not What It Seems

Scripture: "Who against hope believed in hope, that he might become the father of many nations, according to that which was spoken, So shall thy seed be. And being not weak in faith, he considered not his own body now dead, when he was about an hundred years old, neither yet the deadness of Sarah's womb: he staggered not at the promise of God through unbelief; but was strong in faith, giving glory to God;" (Romans 4:18-20 KJV)

**Devotional Message:**

In life, it's easy to look at our circumstances and say, "It is what it is." The natural world presents us with facts: Abraham was old, and Sarah was well past childbearing years. The promise of a child seemed impossible. If we only looked at what was right in front of him, Abraham might have stumbled in his faith. But Romans 4:19 tells us that "he staggered not at the promise of God."

This is a powerful lesson for us. There may be times when our natural circumstances seem to make no sense in light of God's promises. The situation may look one way, but we serve a God of the supernatural. He is the one who "quickeneth the dead, and calleth those things which be not as though they were."

We must be strong in our faith, just as Abraham was. Even when the facts don't add up and the natural things around us look bleak, we must remember that our God is not limited by our reality. He specializes in the impossible. When God shows up, He transforms the "nowhere" into "somewhere." He makes a way where there is no way. What you see is not all there is.

**Reflection Questions:**

- **The God of the Impossible:**

    - What "impossible" situation are you facing right now that you need to surrender to God?
    - How does the example of Abraham's faith encourage you to look past your natural circumstances?

- **Strength in Faith:**

    - In what area of your life do you need to stop "staggering" in unbelief and become strong in faith?
    - How can you give glory to God today by believing in His promise, even when it seems illogical?

**Devotional Prayer:**

Lord, thank You for being the God of the supernatural, who calls things that are not as though they were. Forgive me for the times I have "staggered" in my faith because of what I saw with my natural eyes. Strengthen me to believe in Your promises, even when my circumstances look impossible. Help me to be strong in faith, giving You all the glory. In Jesus' name, Amen.

**Notes:**

_____

_____

_____

# Day 8: His Favor Is Working for Me

Scripture: "And we know that all things work together for good to them that love God, to them who are the called according to his purpose." (Romans 8:28 KJV)

**Devotional Message:**

Life often delivers blows that can leave us weary, broken, and wondering if things will ever get better. But as believers, we have a divine and unshakable assurance: God's favor is always working for us, even when we can't see it or feel it.

Every tear you've shed and every night you've spent awake has been recorded in His book. What felt like a dead end was actually a divine redirection, as the Hand that loves you turns every closed door into a story of redemption. When God is for you, nothing and no one can stand successfully against you. His favor has the power to turn pain into purpose, mourning into dancing, and trials into triumphs.

You may be wrestling with your emotions today, feeling overwhelmed, anxious, or discouraged. But remember that God rules over even your emotions. His Spirit brings a peace that surpasses all understanding and a joy that is not dictated by your circumstances.

Let this be your declaration today:

"This is not the end. His favor is working for me. I will walk in His promises."

You are not forgotten. You are not finished. There will be glory after this.

**Reflection Questions:**

- **Trusting the Process:**

    o    How does the truth that "all things work together for good" change your perspective on a current struggle?

    o    What is one specific situation you are facing right now where you need to believe that God's favor is at work, even if you can't see it?

- **Emotional Peace:**

    o    In what moments do you find yourself wrestling with your emotions? How can you invite God's peace into those moments?

    o    How can you turn a moment of anxiety or discouragement into a declaration of God's favor over your life?

**Devotional Prayer:**

Heavenly Father, thank You for Your unchanging favor. Help me to trust that everything I'm facing is being woven into a greater plan. Strengthen my heart when I feel weak and remind me that even in my struggles, Your favor is still at work. I declare that this is not the end; You are turning it all for my good. In Jesus' name, Amen.

**Notes:**

_____

_____

_____

# Day 9: When Life Doesn't Measure Up to Your Message

Scripture: "I beseech you therefore, brethren, by the mercies of God, that ye present your bodies a living sacrifice, holy, acceptable unto God, which is your reasonable service. And be not conformed to this world: but be ye transformed by the renewing of your mind, that ye may prove what is that good, and acceptable, and perfect, will of God." (Romans 12:1-2 KJV)

**Devotional Message:**

In a generation filled with gifted speakers, influential personalities, and "anointed" voices, it's easy to mistake charisma for consecration. But God is not impressed by how well we preach if we don't live what we preach. Paul's exhortation to the church in Rome wasn't about public performance but about personal presentation. He said, "present your bodies..." This isn't a call to a platform. It is a call to a life.

If your life doesn't measure up to your message, then your message becomes noise, not true ministry. God is calling us beyond a public display into a private discipline. Holiness is not a suggestion. It's a requirement for those who desire to be used by Him. This life must be set apart, not perfect, but presented to God and actively pursuing purity.

Verse 2 reminds us not to be conformed to this world. Too many of us want to be used by God but also want to fit in with the world. The church doesn't need people who are merely capable; it needs people who are willing and available, people who have been transformed and renewed, not just trained and rehearsed.

Being holy and acceptable to God isn't about a title or a platform. It's about your posture before Him. This is our "reasonable service." It's not an extra credit assignment; it's what is expected of us as His followers.

**Reflection Questions:**

- **The Challenge of Consistency:**

  - Is your private life truly lining up with the message you proclaim publicly?

  - In what specific ways are you being "conformed to this world" instead of being "transformed by the renewing of your mind"?

- **Posture and Purpose:**

  - What does it mean for you to present your body as a "living sacrifice"?

  - Are you pursuing holiness in your daily life, or are you primarily seeking a platform or recognition?

**Devotional Prayer:**

Lord, help me to live a life that matches the message You've given me. I surrender myself, mind, body, and spirit as a living sacrifice. I want to be holy, acceptable, and useful for Your glory. Not my will, but Yours be done. In Jesus' Name, Amen.

**Notes:**

_____

_____

_____

# Day 10: Partnering With God for Growth

Scripture: "I planted the seed, Apollos watered it, but God has been making it grow. So neither the one who plants nor the one who waters is anything, but only God, who makes things grow." (1 Corinthians 3:6-7 NIV)

**Devotional Message:**

As believers, we are called to a beautiful partnership with God. The process of growth, whether in our personal lives or in the church, is not an individual effort but a divine collaboration. God calls us to actively sow seeds of faith, nurture those around us, and engage in ministry. However, He alone provides the increase.

Just as a farmer cannot control the rain or the sunshine but must faithfully prepare the soil and plant the seed, we must take intentional steps in our spiritual lives. Personal growth begins with a willingness to be taught and shaped by God. Prayer, studying the Word, and practicing obedience are all ways we prepare our hearts to receive what God wants to do within us.

Similarly, for the church to grow, it requires collaboration between God and His people. Each member must recognize their unique role: some planting seeds by sharing the gospel, others watering by encouraging and teaching, and all working together in unity. In every role, we must never forget that it is God who provides the growth through the power of His Holy Spirit. Our effort is the partnership, His power is the increase.

**Reflection Questions:**

- **Your Role in Growth:**

    o What "seeds" are you currently planting in your own spiritual life and in the lives of others?

    o How can you better collaborate with others in your church or community to work together for growth?

- **Trusting God for the Increase:**

    o Are you focusing more on your own efforts or on trusting God for the growth?

    o What is one step you can take this week to intentionally prepare your heart to receive what God wants to do in your life?

**Devotional Prayer:**

Lord, thank You for the privilege of partnering with You in Your work. Help us to be faithful in planting and watering the seeds You have entrusted to us, trusting that You will bring the increase. Unite us as a church so that we may grow together and glorify You. In Jesus' name, Amen.

**Notes:**

_____

_____

_____

# Day 11: Redeem the Time

Scripture: "Redeeming the time, because the days are evil."
(Ephesians 5:16 KJV)

**Devotional Message:**

Time is a precious and limited gift from God that, once spent, is gone forever. Paul's command to "Redeem the time" is a powerful call to rescue our time from waste and dedicate it to a great and important purpose: advancing the Kingdom of God.

As believers, our lives are not our own, we are called to a mission: to spread Christ's message, serve faithfully, and live boldly for Him. The world is dark, and "the days are evil," meaning the clock is ticking.
We must rise up and stop wasting time on gossip, laziness, or excuses. The world needs what God has placed inside you.

Seize every opportunity God provides:

- Witness when you can.
- Pray when you can.
- Serve when you can.
- Give when you can.

Know God's will by knowing Him personally and intentionally. Today, take a stand in your home, job, and church: speak out! Don't just reclaim your time; reclaim the opportunities, assignments, and purpose God has set before you.

**Reflection Questions:**

- **Stewardship of Time:**

    o   What are some of the biggest distractions or excuses that steal the time you could be using for God's purposes?

    o   What does it look like for you to "walk circumspectly" in your daily life?

- **Action and Obedience:**

    o   In what specific area do you feel God is calling you to "speak out" or "take a stand"?

    o   What is one practical step you can take today to "redeem the time" and be more intentional about your God-given assignment?

**Devotional Prayer:**
Lord, teach us to number our days and to redeem the time You've given us. Open our eyes to see every opportunity to serve, to witness, and to live boldly for You. Help us to be faithful stewards of our time and to walk wisely in this dark world. In Jesus' name, Amen.

**Notes:**

_____

_____

_____

# Day 12: Be Doers, Not Hearers Only

Scripture: "But be ye doers of the word, and not hearers only, deceiving your own selves. For if any be a hearer of the word, and not a doer, he is like unto a man beholding his natural face in a glass: For he beholdeth himself, and goeth his way, and straightway forgetteth what manner of man he was. But whoso looketh into the perfect law of liberty, and continueth therein, he being not a forgetful hearer, but a doer of the work, this man shall be blessed in his deed." (James 1:22-25 KJV)

**Devotional Message:**

Jesus was a man on fire. Everywhere He went, He witnessed, healed, performed miracles, and served the lost. His life was a perfect example of selfless action, driven by love and a desire to see others transformed. Now, let's ask ourselves a challenging question: What have you done lately? Are you living a life of active service or are you more focused on yourself?

James 1:22 tells us not to be mere hearers of the Word but to be doers. It's easy to fall into the trap of being a "mouth saint": quick to talk about faith but slow to live it out. The truth is, our service to others and our sharing of the gospel is a direct reflection of our revelation of Christ. What you truly know about Him will show in how you live for Him.

We are called to be His witnesses, the hands and feet of Jesus in the world today. Our faith isn't meant to be bogged down by our past or our current problems, but always remember that He is the God of the present. What you do for Christ now matters more than just what you say or think. Jesus lived as the perfect example for us, embodying the Word in action, and now it's our turn to follow His lead. Remember, Jesus was the Word made flesh. He didn't just speak about the Kingdom; He lived it. Let's challenge ourselves to do the same, living out our faith in action and making a tangible difference for Christ today.

**Reflection Questions:**

- **From Hearing to Doing:**

  - James says that a hearer who is not a doer "deceives" himself. In what areas of your life might you be hearing the Word but not actively living it out?

  - How does your service to others reflect what you truly know about Christ?

- **An Active Faith:**

  - What is one specific, practical step you can take today to move from being a "hearer only" to a "doer of the work"?

  - Jesus' life was marked by selfless action. How can you challenge yourself to be more selfless and actively serve those around you this week?

**Devotional Prayer:**

Lord, forgive me for the times I have been a hearer of Your Word and not a doer. I ask for a renewed fire within me to live out what I believe. Help me to be Your hands and feet, serving others and sharing Your love. Transform my faith from words into action, so that my life becomes a true reflection of You. In Jesus' name, Amen.

**Notes:**

_____

_____

_____

# Day 13: I Am In Pursuit

Scripture: "But one thing I do: Forgetting what is behind and straining toward what is ahead, I press on toward the goal to win the prize for which God has called me heavenward in Christ Jesus." (Philippians 3:13-14 NIV)

**Devotional Message:**

There comes a critical moment in every believer's life: "Do I stay stuck, or do I move forward?" Despite discouragement, frustration, or the temptation to quit, the divine calling on your life is stronger than the pressure of defeat. Today, declare this boldly: "I am in pursuit. Nothing will stop me." Not fear, fatigue, failure, or past mistakes. Resolve to press toward your purpose, run toward your calling, walk by faith, not by your feelings.

To pursue what God has for you, you must be open to correction, change, and being stretched. You must be vulnerable enough to say, "Lord, I don't have it all together, but I trust You." Be courageous to remove every weight holding you back: the guilt, shame, insecurity, and expectations that were never meant for you. This may require intentionally cutting ties with anything that pulls you back to what God already freed you from. Stay in pursuit.

Now, check your posture. Are you walking with your head held high in faith or bowed low in fear? Are your hands lifted in surrender or clutched around what you're afraid to lose? The enemy wants you to slump into discouragement or sit in stagnation, but you were built to stand and anointed to advance.

This is your season to move with intentionality. Stay focused. Stay prayerful. Stay free. You're not just pursuing *something*, you're pursuing Him. And as you chase after God, everything else will begin to fall into place (Matthew 6:33).

**Reflection Questions:**

- **Past and Future:**

  - Philippians 3:13-14 speaks of "forgetting what is behind." What is one specific thing from your past you need to intentionally forget and leave behind to move forward?

  - What does it mean for you to "press on toward the goal"? What is the goal God has placed before you?

- **Your Posture:**

  - In what area of your life do you feel you're "slumping" into discouragement or doubt?

  - What is one practical step you can take today to change your posture from one of fear to one of faith and surrender?

**Devotional Prayer:**
Lord, I thank You that You have given me a purpose and I choose today to pursue it with everything in me. I ask that You remove every weight, every distraction, and every voice that tries to keep me stuck. Help me to stay open, vulnerable, and postured for progress. I'm not turning back. I'm not slowing down. I am in pursuit of You and everything You've promised. In Jesus' name, Amen.

**Notes:**

_____

_____

_____

# Day 14: You Are Not Defeated

Scripture: "No temptation has overtaken you except what is common to mankind. And God is faithful; he will not let you be tempted beyond what you can bear. But when you are tempted, he will also provide a way out so that you can endure it." (1 Corinthians 10:13 NIV)

**Devotional Message:**

Oftentimes, before our feet even hit the floor in the morning, we allow our thoughts and our present situations to determine the course of the day. But let this serve as a powerful reminder for you today: YOU ARE NOT DEFEATED!

The enemy's greatest desire is for us to walk in defeat. He wants us to focus on what we don't have or to devalue the calling on our lives. But this is your moment to challenge that lie and choose to walk in victory instead of defeat. Instead of defeat, let your response be VICTORY! Today, you can make a choice that changes everything. Declare it now:

- I CHOOSE TO CHANGE MY POSTURE!
- I CHOOSE TO CHANGE MY PERSPECTIVE!
- I CHOOSE VICTORY!

The enemy wants you to fall but remember the promise: "Now unto him that is able to keep you from falling, and to present you faultless before the presence of his glory with exceeding joy, to the only wise God our Saviour, be glory and majesty, dominion and power, both now and ever. Amen." (Jude 1:24)

You have a divine safety net. You are not destined to stumble. Stand firm in your identity and declare it boldly:

- I AM THE HEAD AND NOT THE TAIL!
- I AM THE LENDER AND NOT THE BORROWER!
- I AM A CHILD OF THE KING!
- I AM NOT DEFEAT!

**Reflection Questions:**

- **Choosing Your Mindset:**

    o What negative thoughts or circumstances are you allowing to determine your day before it even begins?

    o How can you intentionally change your posture and perspective to choose victory in a specific situation today?

- **Your Identity:**

    o How does knowing you are a "child of the King" change your response to feelings of defeat?

    o What is one practical step you can take to remind yourself of your identity in Christ throughout your day?

**Devotional Prayer:**
Lord, thank You for the truth that I am not defeated. Forgive me for the times I have allowed my circumstances to overshadow Your promises. Today, I choose victory. Help me to change my posture and my perspective, walking in the authority and power You have given me as Your child. Thank You for being my safety and for providing a way out of every temptation. In Jesus' name, Amen.

**Notes:**

_____

_____

_____

# Day 15: What's In Your Way? What's Your Wall?

Scripture: "By faith the walls of Jericho fell down after they had been encircled for seven days." (Hebrews 11:30, ESV)

**Devotional Message:**

We all come up against insurmountable challenges that leave us feeling exhausted and tempted to give up. These "walls" can block our path in different areas of our lives:

- A marriage where the love has grown cold, despite long and hard fights.
- A longing for healing, even though there's been no sign of improvement.
- The daily burden of a single parent struggling to make ends meet.
- The weary wait for a partner, a child, or a new opportunity.
- The bitterness or unforgiveness that seems impossible to move past.

In these moments of fatigue and fear, it's easy to lower our expectations or even doubt God's plan. But we are reminded of the Israelites at Jericho, who saw a breakthrough not through their own strength but by faith.

You are not alone in facing your wall. The same God who brought down the walls of Jericho is with you, inviting you to put your trust in His power, not your own. Your breakthrough may be closer than you think, waiting for your act of faith.

Don't give up. Continue to believe in God's promises for your life.

**Reflection Questions:**

- What is a "Jericho wall" you are currently facing? What steps have you taken that feel like marching around it?
- How has past perseverance (in any area of your life) prepared you to face your current challenge, even when the outcome isn't yet visible?
- Beyond your own efforts, what "great shout" or "expression of faith" are you being called to make as you wait for your breakthrough?

**Devotional Prayer:**
Heavenly Father, I come to you with my impossible walls, just as your people did at Jericho. Give me the grace to trust in your timing and power, not our own efforts, even when it feels like I am simply marching. I pray that by my faith, you will bring down every obstacle and fulfill your promises in my life. In Jesus' name, Amen.

**Notes:**

_____

_____

_____

# Day 16: Committed In Uncertain Seasons

Scripture: "Let us hold fast the profession of our faith without wavering; (for he is faithful that promised)" (Hebrews 10:23 KJV)

**Devotional Message:**

There are seasons in life when nothing seems to make sense. The road ahead looks unclear, your prayers feel unanswered, and uncertainty tries to whisper fear into your heart. It is in these moments, not in the easy times, that true commitment to God is tested. Faith is not proven when everything is working out, faith is proven when nothing seems to be.

The enemy's strategy in seasons of uncertainty is distraction. He wants you to fix your eyes on the difficulty rather than on God's faithfulness. But Scripture reminds us to "hold fast" to our confession of faith, because the One who promised is faithful. Even when your situation wavers, God does not.

Fear will try to convince you to step back. Faith, however, calls you to stand firm. Fear magnifies the problem. Faith magnifies the promise. Fear creates doubt. Faith builds trust. This is why in moments of confusion, you must denounce fear and declare your faith. Speak God's Word over your situation. Remind your soul that God has never failed you and He will not start now.

Consider Abraham. He didn't know where God was leading him but he stayed committed to the journey. Consider Joseph. His dream didn't make sense while he was in the pit and the prison, but he stayed committed to God's plan. Consider Jesus. In the Garden of Gethsemane, He faced the greatest uncertainty of His earthly life, yet He remained committed to the Father's will.

Don't be distracted by difficulty. Difficulty is not the end, it's often the birthplace of destiny. When you remain committed in uncertain seasons, your faith becomes stronger, your testimony becomes greater, and your trust in God grows deeper.

**Reflection Questions:**

- Focusing on Commitment
  - Where is my "wavering point" right now? What specific uncertainty (a prayer, a relationship, a financial situation) is causing me to be distracted and tempted to loosen my grip on the promises of God?

- Focusing on Faith vs. Fear:
  - Am I currently magnifying the *problem* or the *promise*? What concrete action can I take today (like speaking a specific Bible verse or naming a past faithfulness of God) to denounce fear and intentionally declare my faith over this situation?

- Focusing on Destiny and Difficulty (The Biblical Examples):
  - How can I reframe my current difficulty as a "birthplace of destiny," not an end? What lesson in commitment from the lives of Abraham, Joseph, or Jesus should I adopt to stand firm in this season and allow my faith to grow deeper?

**Devotional Prayer:**
I stand before You today with my impossible walls, trusting You as my Commander. Grant me the grace to commit to Your timing and power, not my own efforts, even when my obedience feels like simple, patient marching. I hold fast to the certainty that You are faithful. By this unwavering faith, I pray You will bring down every obstacle and fulfill Your perfect promises in my life. In Jesus' Name, Amen.

**Notes:**

_____

_____

_____

# Day 17: Unplugged – Disconnect to Reconnect

Scripture: "Do not be misled: 'Bad company corrupts good character.'" (1 Corinthians 15:33 NIV)

**Devotional Message:**

In a world that's constantly plugged in: phones buzzing, social media scrolling, and voices shouting opinions, sometimes the greatest spiritual breakthrough happens when we unplug.

There are seasons when God calls us to disconnect, not out of arrogance, but out of obedience. Some people, places and patterns drain your energy, cloud your discernment, and stifle your growth. Every time you plug into negativity, gossip or chaos, your spirit loses its charge. You can't hear God clearly when too many other frequencies are playing at the same time.

Jesus Himself practiced the art of unplugging. In Luke 5:16, the Bible says, "But Jesus often withdrew to lonely places and prayed." He wasn't avoiding people: He was recharging His purpose. He knew that connection with the Father required disconnection from distraction.

Sometimes the hardest part isn't unplugging from noise, it's unplugging from people who've become crutches. They help you walk for a season, but eventually, they start to limit your movement. If you're not careful, you'll mistake dependency for destiny. God wants to heal your walk, not keep you leaning on others who keep you stuck.

Being unplugged doesn't mean you stop loving people; it means you stop letting the wrong people influence your peace. It means saying, "I can't stay connected to what keeps me disconnected from God."

**Reflection Questions:**

- **Draining Frequencies:** What specific areas or relationships in my life have been draining my energy or peace, making it difficult to hear God clearly?

- **Dependency vs. Destiny:** Have I become dependent on people or patterns that God is now calling me to release in order to step fully into my destiny?

- **The Example of Jesus:** Considering the example of Jesus withdrawing to pray, what is one concrete way I can intentionally unplug from everything this week to truly reconnect with God?

**Devotional Prayer:**

Lord, teach me when to unplug. Help me to disconnect from the things and people that drain my spirit and distract me from Your voice. Give me the strength to walk without crutches and to trust that You are my true source. Recharge me in Your presence and help me live fully connected to You. In Jesus' name, Amen.

**Notes:**

_____

_____

_____

# Day 18: When You Can't Trace God

Scripture: "Trust in the LORD with all your heart and lean not on your own understanding; in all your ways submit to him, and he will make your paths straight." (Proverbs 3:5-6 NIV)

**Devotional Message:**

There is much in this life that we simply don't understand. We face seasons where the reason for a delay, a loss, or a difficult turn remains hidden from our view. It is in these moments, when the path ahead is obscured, and the logic of our situation makes no sense, that our commitment to faith is truly tested.

The enemy will tempt us to rely on our own finite wisdom, urging us to lean on our own understanding (Proverbs 3:5). But Scripture provides an anchor: You can always trust God to direct your path.

Yes, you will have moments when you're tempted to doubt and fear. You may even feel like you've completely lost your way. Yet, the promise remains: "Submit to Him and He will make your paths straight."

Today, remember this powerful truth: Even if you can't trace God's hand, you can always trust His heart. His direction is guaranteed, even when His reasons are not yet revealed.

**Reflection Questions:**

- **Leaning vs. Trusting**
    - In what specific area of my life am I currently tempted to lean on my own understanding (i.e., trying to figure it all out) instead of trusting God's direction?

- **Active Submission**
    - What does it mean practically to "submit" to God in this current situation? Is it through quiet patience, or is it through an act of obedience even when the destination is unclear?

**Devotional Prayer:**

I confess that I often struggle when I cannot trace Your hand or understand Your plans. Forgive me for leaning on my own finite understanding. Today, I surrender my logic and my desire for clarity to Your divine wisdom. I choose to trust You with my whole heart, knowing that You are faithful and good. Direct my path, keep me from stumbling, and help me to rest in the assurance that You are working everything out for my good, even when I cannot see it. In Jesus' name, Amen.

**Notes:**

_____

_____

_____

# Day 19: A Proper Response to God

Scripture: "In every thing give thanks: for this is the will of God in Christ Jesus concerning you." (1 Thessalonians 5:18 KJV)

**Devotional Message:**

God has been too good for us to give Him anything less than a proper response. When we consider all He has done: providing, protecting, forgiving, and sustaining us; it's clear that we owe Him everything.

Yet, how often do we allow circumstances to dictate our response to God? When life is good, we praise Him. When trials arise, we complain or shut down. But Paul reminds us that **thanksgiving isn't optional; it's the will of God.** This means that no matter the situation, our response should always be gratitude.

Giving thanks **in everything** doesn't mean we are thankful *for* everything but that we recognize God's hand **in every situation**. Even in struggles, He is working things together for our good. Our proper response is not just words of thanks, but a life lived in worship, obedience, and trust.

Today, take a moment to reflect: Are you giving God the response He deserves? In trials, will you trust Him? In blessings, will you acknowledge Him? No matter what, let your heart declare, **"Lord, I owe You everything, and I give You thanks!"**

**Reflection Questions:**

- **Response Check:** What is my default response to God when a trial or difficult circumstance arises? Do I quickly move to complaining, or do I first anchor myself in gratitude for His faithfulness?
- **Thanksgiving in Everything:** What is one current struggle or challenge that I can specifically stop and thank God in the midst of, recognizing His hand is still working for my good?
- **Life of Worship:** Beyond saying "thank you," how can I demonstrate a "proper response" to God today through an act of obedience, worship, or renewed trust?

**Devotional Prayer:**

Father, thank You for the truth that You are good and that Your will for me includes gratitude in all things. Forgive me when I allow my emotions, circumstances, or lack of understanding to dictate my response to You. Help me to maintain a steadfast and grateful heart, trusting that You are continually providing, protecting, and working all things together for my ultimate good. I declare today that You deserve my proper response: my life of thanks and obedience. In Jesus' name, Amen.

**Notes:**

_____

_____

_____

# Day 20: His Promises Over My Problems

Scripture: "Then Caleb silenced the people before Moses and said, "We should go up and take possession of the land, for we can certainly do it. But the men who had gone up with him said, "We can't attack those people; they are stronger than we are.""
(Numbers 13:30-31 NIV)

**Devotional Message:**

When faced with challenges, we must choose: Do we trust God's promises, or do we allow fear and doubt to dominate our thinking?

The ten Israelite scouts focused on the giants and the fortified cities, but Caleb and Joshua focused on God's promise.

- **Don't Let "However" Keep You From Your Promise.** The other scouts acknowledged the good land but immediately added, "However, the people are powerful..." That "however" is a spiritual roadblock that shifts your focus from the blessing to the barrier.

- **Faith Over Fear.** Caleb and Joshua saw the same giants but their faith chose to believe that God is greater than any reality. When we focus more on our problems than on God's promises, we forfeit victory.

- **Surround Yourself with Faithful People.** The ten scouts infected the community with fear; you must silence negative voices and surround yourself with people who will remind you of God's power. God's promises are always greater than any problem, and remember, don't be swayed by doubt.

**Reflection Questions:**

- **Identifying the "However":** What current promise of God am I holding onto, but immediately following it with a "however" (a doubt, a fear, or a limitation)?
- **Focus Shift:** Am I currently focusing on the giants (the size of the problem) or the God (the size of the promise)? What is one specific promise I need to declare aloud to shift my focus today?
- **Faithful Influence:** Who are the Calebs and Joshuas in my life—the people who encourage faith? Conversely, what negative voices (social media, news, or individuals) do I need to silence to protect my belief?

**Devotional Prayer:**

Almighty God,

I thank You that Your promises are greater than any barrier. Forgive me for the times I have allowed the "however" of my circumstances to overshadow the certainty of Your Word. Give me the courage of Caleb to silence the fear around me and the faith of Joshua to declare, "We can certainly do it!" Root my conviction in Your power, not my own strength. Surround me with people who speak faith and help me to keep my eyes fixed firmly on Your promises today.

In Jesus' name, Amen.

**Notes:**

---

---

---

# Day 21: Buried but Not Broken

Scripture: "On the first day of the week, very early in the morning, the women took the spices they had prepared and went to the tomb. They found the stone rolled away from the tomb, but when they entered, they did not find the body of the Lord Jesus. While they were wondering about this, suddenly two men in clothes that gleamed like lightning stood beside them. In their fright the women bowed down with their faces to the ground, but the men said to them, "Why do you look for the living among the dead? He is not here; he has risen! Remember how he told you, while he was still with you in Galilee: 'The Son of Man must be delivered over to the hands of sinners, be crucified and on the third day be raised again.'"
(Luke 24:1-7 NIV)

**Devotional Message:**

Sometimes God allows you to be buried in a season but resurrection power is already scheduled. Your season of burying is temporary; you are buried, but not to stay there.
Some of you may be in a season now where you feel like you are being suffocated. Life has been stripped but sometimes we must die to some stuff. It might have started rough, but God specializes in unexpected endings:

- Joseph started in the pit but finished in the palace.
- Job started in suffering but finished with double.
- Jesus started in the grave but finished with all power!

The purpose of Jesus' death and resurrection directly connects to our lives. We must die to self, sin, and old ways. This is the only path to real, abundant life. Jesus was stripped, beaten, and ridiculed, but no matter what He faced, He remained Jesus. His identity was not determined by His suffering. You can be stripped down to the lowest, but it doesn't change who you are in Him.

Christ's resurrection not only secures eternal life but calls us to walk in newness of life, leaving the old self permanently buried. The first Adam failed us, but the Second Adam, Jesus, reconciled us back to the Father. The cross was the darkest day in history, but three days later, Resurrection showed up! We must endure and die to some things, knowing that Resurrection is guaranteed.

**Reflection Questions:**

- **What needs to be buried?** What specific "self," "sin," or "old way" is God asking me to "die to" right now so that new life can be resurrected in me?
- **What is your anchor?** Jesus was stripped down but remained Jesus. What difficult circumstance am I currently facing that is tempting me to forget who I am in Christ, and how can I anchor my identity today?
- **The Guaranteed End:** Reflect on the examples of Joseph, Job, and Jesus. What assurance do I draw from the promise that God specializes in unexpected, victorious endings for those who endure?
- 

**Devotional Prayer:**

Thank You that even when I feel buried, I am not broken, because Your resurrection power is at work in my life. Forgive me for holding onto the old self and the old ways. Today, I surrender my flesh and my self-will, choosing to die to anything that keeps me disconnected from Your abundant life. Give me the strength to endure, knowing that my pain is temporary and my victorious ending is guaranteed in You. Help me to walk in the newness of life You secured through Christ. In Jesus' name, Amen.

**Notes:**

_____

_____

_____

## Notes from the Author

Congratulations on completing *Moments of Refreshing*!

My prayer is that over these 21 days, you've not only found encouragement and peace, but also a divine *refreshing* that renews your strength for the journey ahead. Life has a way of draining us: through responsibilities, struggles, and seasons of waiting but God specializes in restoring what's been depleted.

As you close this devotional, I pray that you don't close your heart to what God has begun. May you rise from this moment renewed in your faith, refocused on your purpose, and ready to fulfill your divine assignment. Remember, refreshing is not a one-time experience, it's a lifestyle of staying connected to the Source.

So, take this renewed strength and go forward with boldness. Walk in purpose. Serve with passion. Live refreshed.

**"He restores my soul; He leads me in the paths of righteousness for His name's sake." — Psalm 23:3**

Stay refreshed,
**Bruce T. Howard, Jr.**

# Acknowledgements

To my **maternal uncles, Wilbur and Wayne,** who were far more than an uncle; you both were a father figure, a steady voice, and a source of strength. Thank you both for being there in ways words could never fully capture.

To my **paternal uncle, Jesse Howard,** affectionately known as Uncle Jake, the jokester, my partner in laughter—though you are no longer here, your memory lives on.

To my **siblings, Brandon, Paris, and Izell III,** thank you for your love, laughter, and unwavering support. May your hearts stay anchored in Christ, and may His purpose continue to unfold in each of your lives.

To my **paternal grandmother, Mrs. Nannie Howard**, thank you for always staying on top of me, pushing me with your humor and love, and helping shape the man I am today.

To my **spiritual parents, Pastor James and Dr. Deborah White**, thank you for covering me, guiding me, and speaking life into my purpose. Your wisdom, prayers, and example have molded my walk with God and fortified my calling.

To my **college advisors, Mrs. Maxine Morant, Dr. Lillie Brugess, Dr. Ronald High, Reverend Thomas Davis, and Reverend Dr. Carlos Brown,** thanks for your guidance and wisdom along the way.

**To my family, maternal, paternal, in-laws, church family,** Jordan Grove C.O.G.I.C.; my extended family, Bishop Mark Walden and the Northern Georgia Second Ecclesiastical Jurisdiction; Superintendent James Bell and the Dublin District C.O.G.I.C., IYD Southeast Region; DCS Behavioral Health Department; Alpha Phi Alpha Fraternity, Inc.; and my friends— thank you. I love you all deeply. Let's always remember to stay refreshed.

www.ingramcontent.com/pod-product-compliance
Lightning Source LLC
Chambersburg PA
CBHW060356130626
46553CB00003B/1255